Working Papers
Volume I, Chapters 1-14

for use with

Financial and
Managerial Accounting:
The Basis for Business Decisions

Twelfth Edition

Jan R. Williams
University of Tennessee - Knoxville

Susan F. Haka
Michigan State University

Mark S. Bettner
Bucknell University

Robert F. Meigs
San Diego State University

 **McGraw-Hill
Irwin**

Boston   Burr Ridge, IL   Dubuque, IA   Madison, WI   New York   San Francisco   St. Louis
Bangkok   Bogotá   Caracas   Kuala Lumpur   Lisbon   London   Madrid   Mexico City
Milan   Montreal   New Delhi   Santiago   Seoul   Singapore   Sydney   Taipei   Toronto

McGraw-Hill Higher Education

A Division of The McGraw-Hill Companies

Working Papers, Volume I, Chapters 1-14 for use with
FINANCIAL AND MANAGERIAL ACCOUNTING: THE BASIS FOR BUSINESS DECISIONS
Jan R. Williams, Susan F. Haka, Mark S. Bettner, Robert F. Meigs

1 2 3 4 5 6 7 8 9 0 CUS/CUS 0 9 8 7 6 5 4 3 2 1

ISBN 0-07-246582-4

www.mhhe.com

Table of Contents

a.

SPENCER MOUNTAIN LODGE					
Balance Sheet					
December 31, 2002					
Assets		Liabilities & Owners' Equity	
		Liabilities:	
		Owners' equity:	

b. _____

_____

_____

_____

_____

2

Description of transactions:

_____
_____
_____
_____
_____
_____
_____
_____
_____
_____

4

PROBLEM 2–3
DELTA COMMUNICATIONS

| | Assets | | | | | | = | Liabilities | | | Owners' Equity |
	Cash	+	Land	+	Building	+	Office Equipment	=	Notes Payable	+	Accounts Payable	+	Capital Stock
December 31 balances	$ 37 000		$ 95 000		$125 000		$ 51 250		$ 80 000		$ 28 250		$ 200 000
(1)												
Balances												
(2)												
Balances												
(3)												
Balances												
(4)												
Balances												
(5)												
Balances												

PROBLEM 2-4
PAULSON TRUCK RENTAL

| | Assets | | | | | = | Liabilities | | Owners' Equity |
	Cash	+	Accounts Receivable	+	Trucks	+	Office Equipment	=	Notes Payable	+	Accounts Payable	+	Capital Stock
December 31 balances	$ 9 5 0 0		$ 8 9 0 0		$ 5 8 0 0 0		$ 3 8 0 0		$ 2 0 0 0 0		$ 5 2 0 0		$ 5 5 0 0 0
(1)													
Balances													
(2)													
Balances													
(3)													
Balances													
(4)													
Balances													
(5)													
Balances													
(6)													
Balances													

a.

HERE COME THE CLOWNS!																	
Balance Sheet																	
June 30, 2002																	
Assets								**Liabilities & Owners' Equity**									
								Liabilities:									
								Owners' equity:									

b. _____

_____

_____

_____

_____

_____

_____

_____

a.

SMOKY MOUNTAIN FARMS						
Balance Sheet						
September 30, 2002						
Assets				Liabilities & Owners' Equity		
				Liabilities:		
				Owners' equity:		

b. _____

_____

_____

_____

_____

_____

_____

a.

THE OVEN BAKERY												
Balance Sheet												
August 1, 2002												
Assets						**Liabilities & Owners' Equity**						
						Liabilities:						
						Owners' equity:						

b.

THE OVEN BAKERY												
Balance Sheet												
August 3, 2002												
Assets						**Liabilities & Owners' Equity**						
						Liabilities:						
						Owners' equity:						

THE OVEN BAKERY						
Statement of Cash Flows						
For the Period August 1–3, 2002						
Cash flows from operating activities:						
Cash flows from investing activities:						
Cash flows from financing activities:						
Cash balance, August 1, 2002						
Cash balance, August 3, 2002						

c. _____

_____

_____

_____

_____

_____

a.

	THE ORIGINAL MALT SHOP													
	Balance Sheet													
	September 30, 2002													
Assets								Liabilities & Owners' Equity						
								Liabilities:						
								Owners' equity:						

b.

	THE ORIGINAL MALT SHOP													
	Balance Sheet													
	October 6, 2002													
Assets								Liabilities & Owners' Equity						
								Liabilities:						
								Owners' equity:						

	THE ORIGINAL MALT SHOP					
	Income Statement					
	For the Period October 1–6, 2002					
Revenues						
Expenses						
Net income						

THE ORIGINAL MALT SHOP Statement of Cash Flows For the Period October 1–6, 2002								
Cash flows from operating activities:								
Cash flows from investing activities:								
Cash flows from financing activities:								
Increase in cash								
Cash balance, October 1, 2002								
Cash balance, October 6, 2002								

c. _____

_____

_____

_____

_____

_____

_____

a.

OLD TOWN PLAYHOUSE								
Balance Sheet								
September 30, 2002								
Assets					Liabilities & Owner's Equity			
					Liabilities:			
					Owners' equity:			

b.

a.

HOLLYWOOD SCRIPTS			
Balance Sheet			
November 30, 2002			
Assets		**Liabilities & Owners' Equity**	
		Liabilities:	
		Owners' equity:	

b. _____

_____

_____

_____

_____

_____

_____

_____

_____

_____

_____

_____

_____

_____

_____

_____

_____

_____

_____

_____

_____

_____

_____

_____

_____

a.

General Journal

20__																		
Feb.	1																	
	10																	
	16																	
	18																	
	22																	
	23																	
	27																	
	28																	

b.

Transaction	Assets	=	Liabilities	+	Owners' Equity
Feb. 1					
Feb. 10					
Feb. 16					
Feb. 18					
Feb. 22					
Feb. 23					
Feb. 27					
Feb. 28					

a. _____

b.

General Journal

20__					
Aug.	1	(1)			
	3	(2)			
	5	(3)			
	17	(4)			
	22	(5)			
	29	(6)			
	30	(7)			

c. _____

d. _____

a.

	Income Statement			Balance Sheet		
Transaction	Revenue	– Expenses	Net = Income	Assets	= Liabilities +	Owners' Equity
Sept. 1						
Sept. 3						
Sept. 9						
Sept. 14						
Sept. 25						
Sept. 26						
Sept. 29						
Sept. 30						

b.

General Journal

Sept.	1			
	3			
	9			
	14			
	25			
	26			
	29			
	30			

c.

NAME _____

SECTION _____ DATE _____

a.

Transaction	Income Statement			Balance Sheet		
	Revenue	– Expenses =	Net Income	Assets	= Liabilities +	Owners' Equity
June 1						
June 2						
June 4						
June 15						
June 15						
June 18						
June 25						
June 30						
June 30						
June 30						
June 30						

b.

		General Journal							
2002									
June	1								
	2								
	4								
	15								
	15								
	18								
	25								
	30								
	30								
	30								
	30								

c.

Date		Explanation	Debit	Credit	Balance
2002					
June	1				
	2				
	4				
	15				
	18				
	25				
	30				

Cash

Date		Explanation	Debit	Credit	Balance
2002					
June	15				
	25				
	30				

Accounts Receivable

Date		Explanation	Debit	Credit	Balance
2002					
June	2				

Aircraft

Date		Explanation	Debit	Credit	Balance
2002					
June	2				

Notes Payable

Date		Explanation	Debit	Credit	Balance
2002					
June	30				

Accounts Payable

Dividends Payable

Date		Explanation	Debit	Credit	Balance
2002					
June	30				

Capital Stock

Date		Explanation	Debit	Credit	Balance
2002					
June	1				

Dividends

Date		Explanation	Debit	Credit	Balance
2002					
June	30				

Aerial Photography Revenue

Date		Explanation	Debit	Credit	Balance
2002					
June	15				
	30				

Maintenance Expense

Date		Explanation	Debit	Credit	Balance
2002					
June	18				

	Fuel Expense			
Date	Explanation	Debit	Credit	Balance
2002				
June 30				

	Salaries Expense			
Date	Explanation	Debit	Credit	Balance
2002				
June 15				
30				

	Rent Expense			
Date	Explanation	Debit	Credit	Balance
2002				
June 4				

d.

AERIAL VIEWS																
Trial Balance																
June 30, 2002																

Total assets:

Total liabilities:

Total stockholders' equity:

**The above figures are most likely not the amounts to be reported
in the balance sheet dated June 30. The accounting cycle includes
adjustments that must be made to the trial balance figures before
financial statements are prepared. The adjusting process is
covered in Chapter 4.**

PROBLEM 3–5
DR. SCHEKTER, DVM

a.

Transaction	Income Statement			Balance Sheet		
	Revenue	– Expenses	= Net Income	Assets	= Liabilities	+ Owners' Equity
May 1						
May 4						
May 9						
May 16						
May 21						
May 24						
May 27						
May 28						
May 31						

b.

			General Journal			
2002						
May	**1**					
	4					
	9					
	16					
	21					
	24					
	27					
	28					
	31					

c.

Cash	Notes Payable

Accounts Receivable	Accounts Payable

Office Supplies	Capital Stock

Medical Instruments	Veterinary Service Revenue

Office Fixtures & Equipment	Advertising Expense

Land	Salary Expense

Building	

d.

DR. SCHEKTER, DVM
Trial Balance
May 31, 2002

e.

Total assets:

Total liabilities:

Total owners' (stockholders') equity:

a.

		General Journal (Adjusting Entries)			
20__		(1)			
Dec	31				
	31	(2)			
	31	(3)			
	31	(4)			
	31	(5)			
	31	(6)			
	31	(7)			
	31	(8)			

b. _____

1. _____
2. _____
3. _____
4. _____
5. _____
6. _____
7. _____
8. _____

c. _____

_____
_____
_____
_____
_____
_____

a.

		General Journal (Adjusting Entries)		
		(1)		
Dec	31			
		(2)		
	31			
		(3)		
	31			
		(4)		
	31			
		(5)		
	31			
		(6)		
	31			
		(7)		
	31			
		(8)		
	31			
		(9)		
	31			

b. _____

1. _____
2. _____
3. _____
4. _____
5. _____
6. _____
7. _____
8. _____
9. _____

c.

	Income Statement			Balance Sheet		
Adjustment	Revenue	− Expenses	= Net Income	Assets	= Liabilities	+ Owners' Equity
1.						
2.						
3.						
4.						
5.						
6.						
7.						
8.						
9.						

d. _____
_____
_____
_____

e. _____
_____
_____
_____
_____
_____

a.   1. _____
_____
_____
_____

   2. _____
_____
_____

   3. _____
_____

   4. _____
_____
_____

b.

General Journal
(Adjusting Entries)

20__		(1)		
June	30			
		(2)		
	30			
		(3)		
	30			
		(4)		
	30			

a.

		General Journal (Adjusting Entries)		
20__		(1)		
Aug.	31			
	31	(2)		
	31	(3)		
	31	(4)		
	31	(5)		
	31	(6)		
	31	(7)		
	31	(8)		
	31	(9)		

b.   1. _____

_____

_____

2. _____

_____

_____

3. _____

c. _____

_____

_____

_____

_____

_____

a.

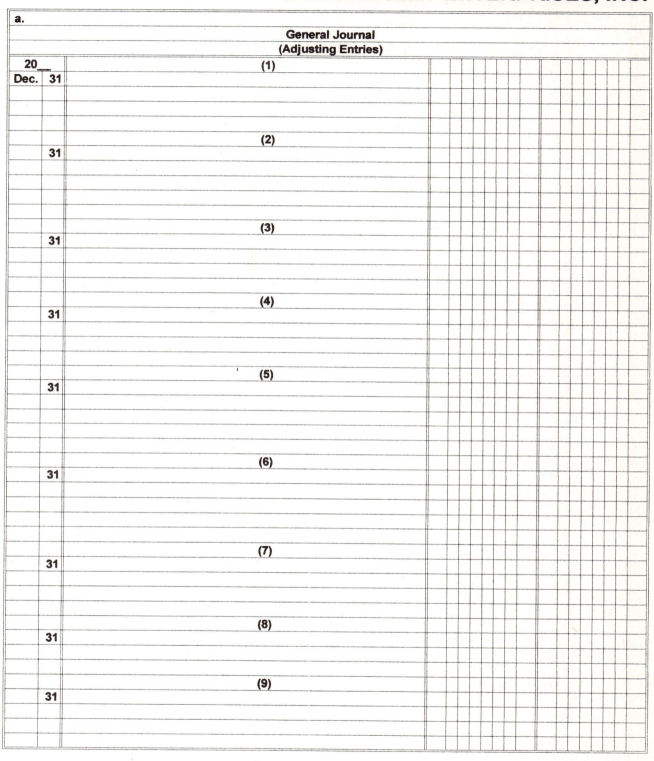

General Journal
(Adjusting Entries)

20__		(1)		
Dec.	31			
	31	(2)		
	31	(3)		
	31	(4)		
	31	(5)		
	31	(6)		
	31	(7)		
	31	(8)		
	31	(9)		

b.

		Ken Hensley Enterprises, Inc.				
		Schedule of Income Earned				
		For the Year Ended December 31, 2002				

c.

	Error	Total Revenue	Total Expenses	Net Income	Total Assets	Total Liabilities	Owners' Equity
a.	Recorded a dividend as an expense reported in the income statement.						
b.	Recorded the payment of an account payable as a debit to accounts payable and a credit to an expense account.						
c.	Failed to record depreciation expense.						
d.	Recorded the issue of capital stock as a debit to cash and a credit to retained earnings.						
e.	Recorded the receipt of a customer deposit as a debit to cash and a credit to fees earned.						
f.	Failed to record expired portion of an insurance policy.						
g.	Failed to record accrued interest earned on an outstanding note receivable.						

b.

	PARTY WAGON, INC.												
	Income Statement												
	For the Year Ended December 31, 2002												
	Revenue:												
	Expenses:												

PARTY WAGON, INC.													
Statement of Retained Earnings													
For the Year Ended December 31, 2002													
Retained Earnings (1/1/02)									$	1	5	0	0	0

PARTY WAGON, INC.				
Balance Sheet				
December 31, 2002				
Assets				
Liabilities				
Stockholders' Equity				

b.

		General Journal		
		(1)		
Dec	31			
		(2)		
		(3)		
		(4)		

c. _____

_____

_____

_____

_____

_____

_____

_____

58

a.

LAWN PRIDE, INC.
Income Statement
For the Year Ended December 31, 2002

Revenue:

Expenses:

LAWN PRIDE, INC.
Statement of Retained Earnings
For the Year Ended December 31, 2002

Retained Earnings (1/1/02)									$	3 0 0 0 0

LAWN PRIDE, INC.										
Balance Sheet										
December 31, 2002										
Assets										
Liabilities										
Stockholders' Equity										

b.

		General Journal										
		(1)										
Dec	31											
		(2)										
		(3)										
		(4)										

c.

LAWN PRIDE, INC.
After-Closing Trial Balance
December 31, 2002

d. _____
_____
_____
_____
_____
_____
_____

a.

	MYSTIC MASTERS, INC.														
	Income Statement														
	For the Year Ended December 31, 2002														
	Revenue:														
	Expenses:														

	MYSTIC MASTERS, INC.								
	Statement of Retained Earnings								
	For the Year Ended December 31, 2002								
	Retained Earnings (1/1/02)						$	2 6 0 0	

a.

MYSTIC MASTERS, INC.

Balance Sheet

December 31, 2002

Assets

Liabilities

Stockholders' Equity

b.

General Journal

		(1)			
Dec	31				
		(2)			
		(3)			
		(4)			

c.

	LAWN PRIDE, INC.		
	After-Closing Trial Balance		
	December 31, 2002		

d. _____
_____
_____
_____
_____
_____
_____
_____

e. _____
_____
_____
_____
_____
_____
_____

a.

GUARDIAN INSURANCE AGENCY Income Statements For the Following Time Periods in 20__	Month Ended Sept. 30	Quarter Ended Sept. 30	9 Months Ended Sept. 30
Revenue:			

b. _____
_____
_____
_____
_____
_____
_____
_____

c. _____
_____
_____
_____
_____
_____
_____
_____
_____
_____

68

b.

		General Journal		
Dec	31	(1)		
		(2)		
		(3)		
		(4)		
		(5)		
		(6)		
		(7)		
		(8)		

a. (continued) *Adjusted trial balance* at December 31, 2002.

BRUSHSTROKE ART STUDIO			
Adjusted Trial Balance			
December 31, 2002			

b.

BRUSHSTROKE ART STUDIO										
Income Statement										
For the Year Ended December 31, 2002										
Revenue:										

BRUSHSTROKE ART STUDIO						
Statement of Retained Earnings						
For the Year Ended December 31, 2002						
Retained Earnings (1/1/02)					$	2 0 0 0 0

b.	BRUSHSTROKE ART STUDIO																
	Balance Sheet																
	December 31, 2002																
	Assets																
	Liabilities																
	Stockholders' Equity																
	TOTAL LIABILITIES AND STOCKHOLDERS' EQUITY																

72

© The McGraw-Hill Companies, Inc., 2002

c.

		General Journal			
Dec	31	(1)			
		(2)			
		(3)			
		(4)			

d.

		BRUSHSTROKE ART STUDIO		
		After-Closing Trial Balance		
		December 31, 2002		

e. _____

_____

_____

_____

_____

_____

_____

_____

a.

General Journal

2002					
Sept	1				
	1				
	1				
	4				
	8				
	12				
	15				
	17				
	23				
	25				

a. (continued)

General Journal

Page 2

2002				
Sept	26			
	27			
	28			
	29			
	29			
	30			
	30			
		(Use General Journal pages 3 and 4, provided at the end of the working papers for this problem, for recording adjusting and closing entries.)		

b.

		Cash				Account No. 1
Date		**Explanation**	**Debit**	**Credit**	**Balance**	
Sept	1					

		Accounts Receivable				Account No. 4
Date		**Explanation**	**Debit**	**Credit**	**Balance**	
Sept	15					

		Prepaid Rent				Account No. 6
Date		**Explanation**	**Debit**	**Credit**	**Balance**	
Sept	1					

		Unexpired Insurance				Account No. 7
Date		**Explanation**	**Debit**	**Credit**	**Balance**	
Sept	29					

		Office Supplies				Account No. 8
Date		**Explanation**	**Debit**	**Credit**	**Balance**	
Sept	4					

Rental Equipment   Account No. 10

Date	Explanation	Debit	Credit	Balance
Sept 1				

Accumulated Depreciation: Rental Equipment   Account No. 12

Date	Explanation	Debit	Credit	Balance
Sept 30				

Notes Payable   Account No. 20

Date	Explanation	Debit	Credit	Balance
Sept 1				

Accounts Payable   Account No. 22

Date	Explanation	Debit	Credit	Balance
Sept 4				

Interest Payable   Account No. 25

Date	Explanation	Debit	Credit	Balance
Sept 30				

	Salaries Payable				Account No. 26
Date	Explanation	Debit	Credit	Balance	
Sept 30					

	Dividends Payable				Account No. 27
Date	Explanation	Debit	Credit	Balance	
Sept 28					

	Unearned Rental Fees				Account No. 28
Date	Explanation	Debit	Credit	Balance	
Sept 8					

	Income Taxes Payable				Account No. 29
Date	Explanation	Debit	Credit	Balance	
Sept 30					

	Capital Stock				Account No. 30
Date	Explanation	Debit	Credit	Balance	
Sept 1					

Retained Earnings — Account No. 35

Date		Explanation	Debit	Credit	Balance
Sept	30				

Dividends — Account No. 38

Date		Explanation	Debit	Credit	Balance
Sept	28				

Income Summary — Account No. 40

Date		Explanation	Debit	Credit	Balance
Sept	30	To close revenue accounts			

Rental Fees Earned — Account No. 50

Date		Explanation	Debit	Credit	Balance
Sept	15				

Salaries Expense — Account No. 60

Date		Explanation	Debit	Credit	Balance
Sept	12				

Maintenance Expense				Account No. 61
Date	**Explanation**	**Debit**	**Credit**	**Balance**
Sept 17				

Utilities Expense				Account No. 62
Date	**Explanation**	**Debit**	**Credit**	**Balance**
Sept 30				

Rent Expense				Account No. 63
Date	**Explanation**	**Debit**	**Credit**	**Balance**
Sept 30				

Office Supplies Expense				Account No. 64
Date	**Explanation**	**Debit**	**Credit**	**Balance**
Sept 30				

		Depreciation Expense																Account No. 65				
Date		Explanation			Debit				Credit					Balance								
Sept	30																						

		Interest Expense																Account No. 66				
Date		Explanation			Debit				Credit					Balance								
Sept	30																						

		Income Taxes Expense																Account No. 67				
Date		Explanation			Debit				Credit					Balance								
Sept	30																						

d.

Tony's Rentals, Inc.			
Income Statement			
For the Month Ended September 30, 2002			
Revenue:			
Expenses:			

Tony's Rentals, Inc.			
Statement of Retained Earnings			
For the Month Ended September 30			
Retained earnings, September 1, 2002			$ -0-

Tony's Rentals, Inc.
Balance Sheet
September 30, 2002

Assets

Liabilities & Owners' Equity

Liabilities:

Stockholders' equity:

Total liabilities and stockholders' equity:

e.

Note 1—Depreciation policies

Note 2—Maturity dates of liabilities

Note 3—Pending litigation

f.

		General Journal (Adjusting Entries)					Page 3	
2002								
Sept	30							
		(Record closing entries on next page.)						

General Journal (Closing Entries)					Page 4	
2002 Sept 30						

g.

Tony's Rentals, Inc.
After-Closing Trial Balance
September 30, 2002

Cash		
Accounts receivable		
Prepaid rent		
Unexpired insurance		
Office supplies		
Rental equipment		
Accumulated depreciation: rental equipment		
Notes payable		
Accounts payable		
Interest payable		
Salaries payable		
Dividends payable		
Unearned rental fees		
Income taxes payable		
Capital stock		
Retained earnings		
Totals		

h. _____

_____

_____

_____

_____

_____

_____

_____

_____

_____

i. _____

_____

_____

_____

_____

_____

_____

a.

General Journal

Nov	5				
	5				
	9				
Dec	5				
	9				
	31				

b.

CLAYPOOL HARDWARE
Partial Income Statement
For the Year Ended December 31, 20___

c. _____

_____

_____

_____

_____

_____

_____

_____

_____

_____

_____

_____

_____

_____

_____

_____

_____

_____

_____

_____

_____

_____

_____

_____

a.

General Journal

May	10				
	23				
	23				
	24				
June	9				
	19				
	19				
	22				

b.

Item	Mitsui P-500 fax machine
Description	Plain paper fax machine
Location	1 in showroom, remainder in warehouse

Primary supplier	Mitsui Corporation
Secondary supplier	None
Inventory level: Minimum	1	Maximum	10

Date	PURCHASED			SOLD			BALANCE		
	Units	Unit Cost	Total	Units	Unit Cost	Total	Units	Unit Cost	Balance
May 10									
23									
24									
June 19									

c. _____

_____

_____

d. _____

_____

_____

_____

_____

_____

_____

_____

_____

	2001–2002	2000–2001
a. 1. Change in net sales		
2. Change in net sales per square foot		
3. Change in comparable store sales		

b.

a.

		General Journal										
Date												
(1)												
June	10											
	15											
	15											
	20											
(2)												
June	10											
	15											
	15											
	20											

b.

(1)												
July	10											
(2)												
July	10											

c.

General Journal

a.		Journal entries by Siogo Shoes:				
Feb	9					
	9					
	12					
	13					
	13					
	19					
b.		Journal entries by Sole Mates:				
Feb.	9					
	12					
	13					

		General Journal									
Feb	19										

c. _____

_____

_____

_____

_____

_____

_____

_____

Parts a, c, g, and h follow; parts b, d, e, and f are on the next page.

a. _____

_____
_____
_____
_____

c. _____

_____
_____
_____
_____
_____
_____
_____
_____

g. _____

_____
_____
_____
_____
_____

h. _____

_____
_____
_____
_____
_____

b.

General Journal

	2002				
Jan	2				
	6				
	6				

d. **Computation of inventory at January 6:**

e. **Journal entries assuming use of a periodic system:**

	2002				
Jan	2				
	6				

f. **Computation of cost of goods sold:**

a.

BANNER, INC.													
Bank Reconciliation													
July 31, 20__													
Balance per bank statement, July 31													
Add:													
Deduct:													
Adjusted cash balance													
Balance per accounting records, July 31													
Add:													
Deduct:													
Adjusted cash balance													

b.

General Journal

20__													
July	31												

c. _____

_____

_____

d. _____

_____

_____

_____

110

a. **Corrected bank reconciliation for November:**
   Balance per bank statement

   Balance per accounting records

b. **Escola attempted to conceal the shortage by making the following intentional errors in her reconciliation:**

c.

a.

Accounts Receivable by Age Group		Percentage Considered Uncollectible	Estimated Uncollectible Accounts
	Amount		
Not yet due		1	
1–30 days past due		3	
31–60 days past due		10	
61–90 days past due		20	
Over 90 days past due		50	
Totals			

b.

General Journal

Dec	31		
c.			
Jan	10		

a.

		General Journal														
2002																
Var.																

b. _____

_____

_____

_____

_____

_____

_____

_____

_____

_____

			Cost	Current Market Value
a.		Current assets:		
		Stockholders' equity:		
b.				
Apr	10			
Aug	7			
c.		Marketable Securities account:		
d.				
e.				
f.		Current assets:		
		Stockholders' equity:		

g. Nonoperating Items:						

h.

General Journal

20__								
Sept	1							
Dec	31							
June	1							
b.		Assuming that note was defaulted.						
20__								
June	1							

c. _____
_____
_____
_____
_____

a.

		General Journal				
2002						
		(1) Specific identification method:				
Jan	15					
		(2) Average-cost method:				
Jan	15					
		(3) First-in, first-out (FIFO) method:				
Jan	15					
		(4) Last-in, first-out (LIFO) method:				
Jan	15					

BASSTRACK (continued)

b. Inventory subsidiary ledger records:

(1) Specific identification method:

Date	PURCHASED Units	PURCHASED Unit Cost	PURCHASED Total	SOLD Units	SOLD Unit Cost	SOLD Cost of Goods Sold	BALANCE Units	BALANCE Unit Cost	BALANCE Balance
Dec 12									
Jan 9									
Jan 15									

(2) Average-cost method:

Date	PURCHASED Units	PURCHASED Unit Cost	PURCHASED Total	SOLD Units	SOLD Unit Cost	SOLD Cost of Goods Sold	BALANCE Units	BALANCE Unit Cost	BALANCE Balance
Dec 12									
Jan 9									
Jan 15									

(3) First-in, first-out (FIFO) method:

Date	PURCHASED Units	PURCHASED Unit Cost	PURCHASED Total	SOLD Units	SOLD Unit Cost	SOLD Cost of Goods Sold	BALANCE Units	BALANCE Unit Cost	BALANCE Balance
Dec 12									
Jan 9									
Jan 15									

(4) Last-in, first-out (LIFO) method:

Date	PURCHASED Units	PURCHASED Unit Cost	PURCHASED Total	SOLD Units	SOLD Unit Cost	SOLD Cost of Goods Sold	BALANCE Units	BALANCE Unit Cost	BALANCE Balance
Dec 12									
Jan 9									
Jan 15									

c. _____
_____
_____
_____
_____

a. **Cost of goods sold and ending inventory**

(1) **Average-cost method:**

(2) **First-in, first-out (FIFO) method:**

(3) **Last-in, first-out (LIFO) method:**

b.   (1) _____

_____

_____

_____

    (2) _____

_____

_____

_____

    (3) _____

_____

_____

_____

a.

1.   Average-cost method:

2.   First-in, first-out (FIFO) method:

3.   Last-in, first-out (LIFO) method:

b. _____

_____

_____

_____

_____

NAME _____

SECTION _____ DATE _____

a.	Shrinkage loss -- 50 trees						
(1)	Average-cost method:						

(2)	Last-in, first-out (LIFO) method:						

b.	Shrinkage loss and LCM adjustment						
(1)	Shrinkage loss, first-in, first-out (FIFO) method:						

(2)	Write-down of inventory to the lower-of-cost-or-market:						

c. _____

_____

_____

_____

_____

	Units	Unit Cost	Total Cost
a. Inventory and cost of goods sold:			
(1) FIFO:			
(2) LIFO:			
(3) Average cost:			

b. _____

_____

_____

_____

_____

_____

_____

a.

	2002	2001	2000
Net sales			
Cost of goods sold			
Gross profit on sales			
Gross profit percentage			

b. _____

_____

_____

_____

_____

_____

a.

  (1) Estimated cost of goods sold:

  (2) Estimated ending inventory:

b.

  (1) Restating physical inventory from retail prices to cost:

  (2) Estimated shrinkage losses at cost:

  (3) Computation of gross profit:

c.

a.

GUITAR UNIVERSE, INC.					
Bank Reconciliation					
December 31, 2002					
Balance per bank statement, December 31, 2002					$ 4 6 9 7 5

General Journal		
a.		
b.		
c.		
d.		
e.		

		General Journal					
f.							
g.							
h.							
i.							

j.

GUITAR UNIVERSE, INC.		
Adjusted Trial Balance		
As of December 31, 2002		

k.

GUITAR UNIVERSE, INC.
Income Statement
For the Year Ending December 31, 2002

Sales							$16032 00

GUITAR UNIVERSE, INC.
Statement of Retained Earnings
For the Year Ending December 31, 2002

Beginning Retained Earnings (January 1, 2001)						$2402 00

k. (continued)	GUITAR UNIVERSE, INC.		
	Balance Sheet		
	As of December 31, 2002		
Assets			
Current assets:			
Plant and equipment:			
Liabilities			
Current liabilities:			
Long-term liabilities:			
Stockholders' Equity			

l. Step 1: Compute accounts receivable turnover (sales ÷ accounts receivable)

Step 2: Compute accounts receivable days (365 ÷ accounts receivable turnover)

m. Step 1: Compute inventory turnover (cost of goods sold ÷ merchandise inventory)

Step 2: Compute inventory days (365 ÷ inventory turnover)

n.

o.

a.

b.

c.	Expenditures that should be debited to the Computing								
	Equipment account:								

d.

General Journal

Dec	31								

a. (1) Straight-Line Schedule:

Year	Computation	Depreciation Expense	Accumulated Depreciation	Book Value
2001				
2002				
2003				
2004				
2005				
2006				

(2) 200% Declining-Balance Schedule:

Year	Computation	Depreciation Expense	Accumulated Depreciation	Book Value
2001				
2002				
2003				
2004				
2005				
2006				

(3) 150% Declining-Balance Schedule:

Year	Computation	Depreciation Expense	Accumulated Depreciation	Book Value
2001				
2002				
2003				
2004				
2005*				
2006*				

* Switch to straight-line

b.

_____

_____

_____

_____

_____

_____

c. Computation of gains or losses upon disposal:

1. Straight-Line

2. 200% Declining-Balance:

3. 150% Declining-Balance:

a. Costs to be depreciated include:

(1) Straight-Line (nearest whole month):

Year	Computation	Depreciation Expense	Accumulated Depreciation	Book Value
2001				
2002				
2003				
2004				

(2) 200% Declining-Balance (half-year convention):

Year	Computation	Depreciation Expense	Accumulated Depreciation	Book Value
2001				
2002				
2003				
2004				

(3) 150% Declining-Balance (half-year convention):

Year	Computation	Depreciation Expense	Accumulated Depreciation	Book Value
2001				
2002				
2003				
2004				

b. _____

_____

_____

_____

_____

c. _____

_____

_____

_____

d. _____

_____

_____

1. Journal entries assuming that the shelving was sold for $1,000:

2. Journal entries assuming that the shelving was sold for $300:

a.

General Journal

Feb	10					
Apr	1					
Aug	15					
Oct	1					

b. _____

_____

_____

_____

c. _____

_____

_____

_____

a. _____
_____
_____
_____

b. _____
_____
_____
_____
_____

c. _____
_____
_____
_____
_____

d. _____
_____
_____
_____

e. _____
_____
_____
_____

a. Estimated goodwill associated with the purchase of Phil's Garage:

b. Estimated goodwill associated with the purchase of Gas N'Go:

c.

_____
_____
_____
_____
_____
_____
_____
_____
_____

PROBLEM 10—1
COMPUTER SPECIALISTS, INC.

Income Statement

Transaction	Revenue	—	Expenses	=	Net Income
a					
b					
c					
d					
e					
f					
g					
h					
i					
j					
k					
l					
*m					
*n					
*o					

Balance Sheet

Assets	=	Current Liabilities	+	Long-Term Liabilities	+	Owners' Equity

*Supplemental Topic A, "Estimated Liabilities, Loss Contingencies, and Commitments."

© The McGraw-Hill Companies, Inc., 2002

a.

SEATTLE CHOCOLATES Partial Balance Sheet December 31, 2002				
Liabilities:				
Current liabilities:				
Long-term liabilities:				
Total liabilities				

b. Comments on information in the numbered paragraphs:

   (1) _____

_____

_____

   (2) _____

_____

_____

_____

   (3) _____

_____

   (4) _____

_____

_____

_____

_____

a.

	General Journal				
20__					
Aug 6					
Sept 16					
Sept 20					
Nov 1					
Dec 1					
Dec 16					
b.	**Adjusting Entry**				
Dec 31					

c. _____

_____

_____

a. and d.

a. _____
_____
_____
_____
_____
_____

d. _____
_____
_____
_____
_____
_____
_____
_____
_____

b.

General Journal

2002						
Oct	1					
Nov	1					

c.

Amortization Table
(12%, 30-Year Mortgage Note Payable for $1,080,000;
Payable in 360 Monthly Installments of $11,110)

Interest Period	Payment Date	Monthly Payment	Interest Expense	Reduction in Unpaid Balance	Unpaid Balance
Issue date	Sept. 1, 2002	—	—	—	$1 080 000
1	Oct. 1				
2	Nov. 1				
3	Dec. 1				
4	Jan. 1, 2003				

General Journal

a.					
2002					
Aug	1				
b.					
Nov	1				
c.					
Dec	31				
d.					
2003					
May	1				

e. _____

_____

_____

_____

a.

		General Journal																		
(1)		**Bonds issued at 98:**																		
2002																				
Dec	31																			
2003																				
Mar	1																			
(2)																				
2002																				
Dec	31																			
2003																				
Mar	1																			

b.		Net bond liability at Dec. 31, 2003:	Bonds Issued at 98	Bonds Issued at 101
		Bonds payable		
	*	Less: Discount on bonds payable		
	**	Add: Premium on bonds payable		
		Net bond liability		

* **Computation of discount amortized at Dec. 31, 2003:**

** **Computation of premium amortized at Dec. 31, 2003:**

c. _____

_____

_____

_____

a.

MINNESOTA SATELLITE TELEPHONE CORPORATION
Partial Balance Sheet
December 31, 2002

(in thousands)

Liabilities:
 Current liabilities:

Long-term liabilities:

Part *b* appears on the following page.

c. **(1)**

(2)

Part *d* appears on the following page.

b.   (1) _____

_____

_____

_____

(2) _____

_____

_____

(3) _____

_____

_____

_____

(4) _____

(5) _____

_____

_____

(6) _____

_____

d. _____

_____

_____

_____

_____

_____

_____

_____

_____

a.

SINCLAIR PRESS
Partial Balance Sheet
December 31, 2002

Stockholders' equity

b. _____

_____

_____

_____

_____

_____

_____

_____

c. _____

_____

_____

a.

BANNER PUBLICATIONS								
Partial Balance Sheet								
December 31, 2002								
Stockholders' equity:								

b. _____

_____

_____

_____

_____

c. _____

_____

_____

_____

172

NAME _____

SECTION _____ DATE_____

MANHATTAN TRANSPORT COMPANY

a.

MANHATTAN TRANSPORT COMPANY		
Partial Balance Sheet		
December 31, 2002		

Stockholders' equity:

b. _____

_____

_____

_____

_____

_____

_____

_____

_____

_____

_____

a.

General Journal

20__					
Jan	6				
	7				
	12				
June	4				
Nov	15				
Dec	20				
	31				
	31				

b.

MOBILE COMMUNICATIONS, INC.
Partial Balance Sheet
December 31, 20__

Stockholders' equity:

a.

b.

c.

d.

e.

f.

g.

h.

	In Thousands (Except for Per Share Amounts)
a.	
b.	
c.	
d.	

e.

f.

g.

NAME _____

SECTION _____ DATE _____

a. _____

_____

_____

_____

_____

_____

_____

_____

_____

_____

_____

b. _____

_____

_____

_____

_____

_____

_____

_____

_____

_____

_____

_____

_____

_____

a.

Stockholders' equity:			

b. _____

_____

_____

c. _____

_____

_____

_____

a. Stockholders' equity:

b. _____

c. _____

a.

ATLANTIC AIRLINES
Income Statement
For the Year Ended December 31, 20__

b. Estimated earnings per share next year:

NAME _____

SECTION_____ DATE _____

a.

ASHTON SOFTWARE, INC.
Condensed Income Statement
For the Year Ended December 31, 2002

Net Sales

Earnings per share:

b.

ASHTON SOFTWARE, INC.
Statement of Retained Earnings
For the Year Ended December 31, 2002

c.

d.

a.

ASPEN, INC.

Income Statement

For the Year Ended December 31, 2002

Net Sales

Earnings per share of capital stock:

b.

ASPEN, INC. Statement of Retained Earnings For the Year Ended December 31, 2002				

c.

	Total Stockholders' Equity	Number of Shares Outstanding	Book Value Per Share
Beginning balance			
Jan. 10			
Mar. 15			
May 30			
July 31			
Dec. 15			
Dec. 31			

PROBLEM 12–5

MARBLE OASIS CORPORATION

MARBLE OASIS CORPORATION
Statement of Stockholders' Equity
For the Year Ended December 31, 20___

a.

	Capital Stock ($10 par value)	Additional Paid-In Capital	Retained Earnings	Treasury Stock	Total Stockholders' Equity

(part *b* is on following page)

b.

a.

General Journal				
2002				
Jan	3			
Feb	15			
Apr	12			
May	9			
June	1			
	30			
Aug	4			
Dec	31			
Dec	31			

b.

OVERNIGHT LETTER
Partial Balance Sheet
December 31, 2002

Stockholders' equity:

c. **Computation of maximum legal cash dividend per share at**
   December 31, 2002:

a.

Event	Current Assets	Stockholders' Equity	Net Income	Net Cash (from Any Source)
——	——	——	——	——
——	——	——	——	——
——	——	——	——	——
——	——	——	——	——
——	——	——	——	——

I = Increase   D = Decrease   NE = No effect

b.   **(1)** _____

_____

_____

_____

_____

(2) _____

_____

_____

_____

(3) _____

_____

_____

_____

(4) _____

_____

_____

_____

_____

_____

(5) _____

_____

_____

_____

_____

_____

_____

a.

MANDELLA CORPORATION
Partial Balance Sheet
December 31, 2001

Stockholders' equity:

b.

MANDELLA CORPORATION
Partial Balance Sheet
December 31, 2002

Stockholders' equity:

a.

FALLON MANUFACTURING CORPORATION						
Partial Income Statement					(Dollars in	
For the Year Ended December 31, 20__					Thousands)	
Loss from continuing operations						

b.

a. _____

b. _____

c. _____

d. _____

e. _____

f. _____

g. _____

_____

h. _____

i. _____

_____

j. _____

k. _____

l. _____

m. _____

n. _____

_____

o. _____

_____

_____

206

REIZENSTEIN COMPANY		
Statement of Cash Flows		
For the Year Ended December 31, 2002		
Cash flows from operating activities:		
Cash flows from investing activities:		
Cash flows from financing activities:		
Net increase (decrease) in cash and cash equivalents		
Cash and cash equivalents, beginning of year		
Cash and cash equivalents, end of year		
Supporting computations:		

208

a.

FELLINI FASHIONS

Partial Statement of Cash Flows

For the Year Ended December 31, 2002

Cash flows from investing activities:

Supporting computations:

b.

Schedule of noncash investing and financing activities:

c. _____

_____

_____

_____

_____

a.

XAVIER IMPORTS
Partial Statement of Cash Flows
For the Year Ended December 31, 2002

Cash flows from investing activities:

Supporting computations:

  (1) Proceeds from sales of marketable securities:

  (2) Proceeds of noncash investing and financing activities:

b. Schedule of noncash investing and financing activities:

c.

a.

JUAREZ INTERIORS, INC.
Partial Statement of Cash Flows
For the Year Ended December 31, 2002

Cash flows from operating activities:

b.

JUAREZ INTERIORS, INC.						
Partial Statement of Cash Flows						
For the Year Ended December 31, 2002						
Cash flows from operating activities:						
Net income					$203000	

a.

MILLENNIUM TECHNOLOGIES
Statement of Cash Flows
For the Year Ended December 31, 2002

Cash flows from operating activities:

Cash flows from investing activities:

Cash flows from financing activities:

Net increase (decrease) in cash and cash equivalents
Cash and cash equivalents, beginning of year
Cash and cash equivalents, end of year

Supporting computations:

Supporting computations:

b. _____
_____
_____
_____
_____
_____
_____
_____
_____

c. _____
_____
_____
_____

a.

SPACENET 2010
Worksheet for a Statement of Cash Flows
For the Year Ended December 31, 2002

Balance sheet effects:	Effects of Transactions			
	Beginning Balance	Debit Changes	Credit Changes	Ending Balance
Assets				
Cash and cash equivalents				
Liabilities & Owners' Equity				

Cash effects:	Sources	Uses	
Operating activities:			
Investing activities:			
Financing activities:			
Net decrease in cash			
Totals			

b.

SPACENET 2010				
Statement of Cash Flows				
For the Year Ended December 31, 2002				
Cash flows from operating activities:				
Net income				$ 440000
Cash flows from investing activities:				
Cash flows from financing activities:				
Net increase (decrease) in cash				
Cash and cash equivalents, Dec. 31, 2001				
Cash and cash equivalents, Dec. 31, 2002				
Supplementary Schedule: Noncash Investng & Financing Activities				

c. _____
_____
_____
_____
_____
_____
_____
_____
_____
_____
_____
_____

d. _____
_____
_____

a.

WONDER TOOL, INC.
Worksheet for a Statement of Cash Flows
For the Year Ended December 31, 2002

Balance sheet effects:	Effects of Transactions			
	Beginning Balance	Debit Changes	Credit Changes	Ending Balance
Assets				
Cash and cash equivalents				
Liabilities and Owners' Equity				
Cash effects:		Sources	Uses	
Operating activities:				
Investing activities:				
Financing activities:				
Net increase in cash				
Totals				

b.	WONDER TOOL, INC.											
	Statement of Cash Flows											
	For the Year Ended December 31, 2002											
Cash flows from operating activities:												
Net loss									$	(34000)		
Cash flows from investing activities:												
Cash flows from financing activities:												
Net incrase in cash												
Cash and cash equivalents, Dec. 31, 2001												
Cash and cash equivalents, Dec. 31, 2002												
Supplementary Schedule: Noncash Investing & Financing Activities												

c. _____

_____

_____

_____

_____

_____

_____

_____

_____

_____

_____

_____

_____

d. _____

_____

_____

_____

_____

_____

_____

_____

_____

e. _____

_____

_____

_____

f. _____

_____

_____

_____

_____

_____

_____

If management decides to continue business operations, it should take the following actions:

a. Common size income statement:	Sub Zero, Inc.	Industry Average
Sales (net)	1 0 0 %	1 0 0 %

b. _____

_____

_____

_____

_____

_____

_____

_____

_____

_____

_____

_____

_____

_____

_____

_____

_____

_____

_____

_____

_____

_____

_____

_____

_____

_____

230

	2002	2001
a. Net sales:		
b. Cost of goods sold in dollars:		
Cost of goods sold as a percentage of net sales:		
c. Operating expenses in dollars:		
Operating expenses as a percentage of net sales:		

d.

CUSTOM LOGOS, INC.
Condensed Comparative Income Statement
For the Years Ended December 31, 2002 and December 31, 2001

	2002	2001

e.

a.   **Current assets:**

Current liabilities:

b. _____

_____

_____

_____

_____

_____

_____

_____

_____

_____

	(Dollars in Millions)			
a. **Current assets:**				
Cash	$	7 4	.	8
Quick assets:				
b. **(1)** **Current ratio:**				
(2) **Quick ratio:**				
(3) **Working capital:**				

c. _____

_____

_____

_____

_____

d. _____

_____

_____

_____

_____

_____

_____

_____

e. _____

_____

_____

_____

			(Dollars in Thousands)
a. **(1) Quick assets:**			
Cash			$ 4 7 5 2 4
(2) Current assets:			
(3) Current liabilities:			
b. **(1) Quick ratio:**			
(2) Current ratio:			
(3) Working capital:			
(4) Debt ratio:			

c.   (1)

    (2)

    (3)

Parts *a, c, e,* and *f* appear on the following page.

b. **(1)** **Current ratio:**

      Current assets:

(2) **Quick ratio:**

(3) **Working capital:**

(4) **Debt ratio:**

d. **(1)** **Return on assets:**

(2) **Return on equity:**

a.

c.

e.

f. (1)

(2)

a. Computation of quick assets, current assets, and current liabilities
at the beginning of the year:

Quick assets:

Current assets:

Current liabilities:

b. Computation of current ratio, quick ratio, and working capital:

(1) Current ratio

(2) Quick ratio

(3) Working capital

c. **Effect of transactions:**

	Effect on			
Item	**Current Ratio**	**Quick Ratio**	**Working Capital**	**Net Cash Flow from Operating Activities**
0. Sold inventory on account at a loss	Decrease	Increase	Decrease	No Effect
1. Issued capital stock for cash				
2. Sold temporary investments at a loss				
3. Acquired temporary investments				
4. Wrote off uncollectible accounts				
5. Sold inventory on account at a gain				
6. Acquired plant and equipment for cash				
7. Declared a cash dividend				
8. Declared a 10% stock dividend				
9. Paid accounts payable				
10. Purchased goods on account				
11. Collected cash on accounts receivable				
12. Borrowed cash on a short-term note				

a. (1)

BARKER DEPARTMENT STORE Balance Sheet December 31, 2001									(Dollars in Thousands)							
Assets																
Liabilities & Stockholders' Equity																

Supporting computations:

a. (2)

BARKER DEPARTMENT STORE Income Statement For the Year Ended December 31, 2001		(Dollars in Thousands)
Net sales		$10000

Supporting computations:

		(Dollars in Thousands)
b. (1) Current ratio:		
(2) Working capital:		
c. (1) Gross profit rate:		
(2) Return on total assets:		
(3) Return on stockholders' equity:		

d. _____

_____

_____

_____

_____

_____

_____

_____

_____

_____

_____

	(Dollar Amounts in Thousands)
a. **Current ratio:**	
(1) Beginning of year	
(2) End of year	
b. **Working capital:**	
(1) Beginning of year	
(2) End of year	
d. (1) Return on average total assets:	
(2) Return on average stockholders' equity:	

c. and e.

c. _____

_____

_____

_____

_____

_____

_____

_____

_____

_____

_____

e. _____

_____

_____

_____

_____

a. (1) Inventory turnover:

(2) Accounts receivable turnover:

(3) Total operating expenses:													

(4) Gross profit percentage:

(5) Return on average stockholders' equity:

(6) Return on average assets:													

b.

a.

	Another World	Imports, Inc.
(1) Working capital:		
(2) Current ratio:		
(3) Quick ratio:		
(4) Number of times inventory turned over during the year:		
Average number of days required to turn over inventory:		
(5) Number of times accounts receivable turned over:		
Average number of days required to collect accounts receivable:		
(6) Operating cycle:		

b.
_____

a.

	Goodyear	Goodrich
(1) Current ratio:		
(2) Quick ratio:		
(3) Working capital (dollar amounts in thousands):		
(4) Return on average total assets:		
(5) Return on average total stockholders' equity:		

b. _____

_____

_____

_____

_____

_____

_____

c. _____

_____

_____

_____

_____

_____

(1) _____

(2) _____
_____

(3) _____
_____

(4) _____
_____

(5) _____

(6) _____
_____

(7) _____
_____

(8) _____
_____

(9) _____
_____

(10) _____
_____
_____

(11) _____
_____

(12) _____
_____
_____

a. _____
_____
_____
_____
_____
_____
_____
_____
_____
_____

b. _____
_____
_____
_____
_____
_____
_____
_____
_____
_____
_____

c. _____
_____
_____
_____
_____
_____
_____
_____
_____
_____
_____

d. _____

_____

_____

_____

_____

_____

_____

_____

_____

_____

e. _____

_____

_____

_____

_____

_____

_____

_____

_____

_____

f. _____

_____

_____

_____

_____

_____

_____

_____

_____

_____

	(Dollars in Thousands) For the Years Ended	
	Dec. 31, 1999	Dec. 31, 1998
a. **(1)** **Current ratio:**		
(2) **Quick ratio:**		
(3) **Working capital:**		
(4) **Percentage change in working capital:**		
(5) **Percentage change in cash:**		

b. _____

_____

_____

_____

_____

_____

_____

_____

c. _____

_____

_____

_____

_____

_____

_____

d. _____

_____

_____

_____

_____

_____

_____

_____

e. _____

_____

_____

_____

_____

_____

_____

_____

	(Thousands of Dollars) For the Years Ended	
	Dec. 31, 1999	Dec. 31, 1998
a. (1) Percentage change in net sales:		
(2) Percentage change in net earnings:		
(3) Gross profit rate:		
(4) Net income as percentage of sales:		
(5) Return on average assets:		
Average total assets:		
Return on average assets (earnings from operations/ average assets):		
(6) Return on average total equity:		

	(Dollars in Thousands) For the Years Ended	
	Dec. 31, 1997	Dec. 31, 1998
(6) Return on average total equity:		
Average stockholders' equity:		
Return on average stockholders' equity:		

b. _____
_____
_____
_____
_____
_____
_____
_____
_____
_____
_____
_____
_____
_____
_____
_____
_____
_____
_____
_____
_____
_____
_____